NELSON MANDELA

■ ■ ■ ■ ■ ■

Katherine Tegen Books is an imprint of HarperCollins Publishers.

Nelson Mandela
Copyright © 2013 by Kadir Nelson
All rights reserved. Manufactured in China.
No part of this book may be used or reproduced in any manner whatsoever without written permission except in the case of
brief quotations embodied in critical articles and reviews. For information address HarperCollins Children's Books, a division
of HarperCollins Publishers, 10 East 53rd Street, New York, NY 10022.
www.harpercollinschildrens.com

Library of Congress Cataloging-in-Publication Data is available.
ISBN 978-0-06-178374-6 (trade bdg.) — ISBN 978-0-06-178376-0 (lib. bdg.)
ISBN 978-0-06-224636-3 (intl. ed.)

Typography by Martha Rago
13 14 15 16 17   SCP   10 9 8 7 6 5 4 3 2 1
❖
First Edition

NELSON MANDELA

WORDS AND PAINTINGS BY

KADIR NELSON

KATHERINE TEGEN BOOKS

An Imprint of HarperCollins Publishers

Rolihlahla played barefooted
on the grassy hills of Qunu.
He fought boys with sticks
and shot birds with slingshots.
The smartest Madiba child of thirteen,
he was the only one chosen for school.
His new teacher would not say his Xhosa name.
She called him Nelson instead.

Nelson was nine when his father
joined the ancestors in the sky.
To continue his schooling,
Nelson was sent miles away
to live with a powerful chief.
"Brace yourself, my boy."
His mother held her tears
and said good-bye.

The chief held counsel to warriors,
medicine men, farmers, and laborers.
The elder ones told stories of old Africa.

For centuries

Thembu, Pondo, Xhosa, and Zulu peoples

lived in the mountains and valleys of South Africa.

The land was bountiful, fertile, and rich.

The people hunted, fished, and raised crops, living in relative peace.

But they made war on European settlers

who came in search of land and treasure.

The settlers' weapons were stronger and breathed fire.

Slowly, the people were conquered.

Their land was taken and spirits dimmed.

South Africa belonged to Europe.

The elders grew quiet and Nelson felt sorry.

Nelson grew into a young man
and attended fine schools
in the golden city of Johannesburg,
where Africans were poor
and powerless.
Nelson became a lawyer
and defended those
who could not defend themselves.

The government grew harsh
and created a cruel policy.
It split the people in three—
African. Indian. European.
It was called apartheid.
The people were set apart.
"European Only" beaches.
"European Only" parks.
"European Only" theaters.
And the people protested.

Nelson organized rallies
to fight apartheid.
"We must win back Africa," he told them.
"South Africa is for all South Africans."
"Amandla!" he shouted.
"Ngawethu!" they responded.
Power to the people!
And the people loved him.

Speaking out was against the law
and Nelson was arrested and jailed
for a fortnight with a hundred men.
They danced and sang,
calling the ancestors
to join the fight for freedom.

Amandla!
Ngawethu!

The ancestors sent their daughter Winnie
to stand next to Nelson.
They found love and married
and welcomed children into the world.
Together they stood
and fought apartheid.

The state vowed to put Nelson in jail
and he went underground.
He wore different disguises
and lived in the shadows.
Empty flats, farmhouses, and
bedrooms of friends became Nelson's home
while he organized more rallies and protests.
The police put out a warrant for his arrest
but they could not find him.

Nelson slipped across the border to visit free nations
where black Liberians, Ethiopians, and Moroccans
freely conversed with white Europeans
and brown Egyptians.
They shook hands—
a glimpse of freedom for life at home.
Nelson returned to South Africa
to cleanse his homeland of hate and discrimination.

With a vision for peace and harmony,
Nelson felt renewed and ready
to fight for freedom.
But on a drive to town
he was captured,
arrested, and taken to jail.
The people cried
"Free Mandela,"
"Free Mandela."
Wet paint
and posters
covered South African walls.

On a small island off the coast
of the southern tip of Africa,
Nelson sat in a tiny cell.
Every day
the world passed him by.
Cold mealies, thin blankets, hard labor.
Nelson hammered rocks into dust, and
read, studied, and educated fellow prisoners.
Days turned into weeks, months, and years.

His children grew up.

Relatives passed away.

South Africa began to fall apart.

There were more protests,

more rallies,

and violence.

The people needed a leader.

Nelson snuck a message to the people:

"I will return."

As years passed,
the world pressed South Africa to change.
The new president agreed,
and "European Only" signs came down.
Beaches, parks,
and theaters opened.
Nelson's comrades were set free.
Apartheid was no more.

Nelson was an old man.
After twenty-seven and one-half years,
the prison gates opened
and Nelson was at last
set free.
Thousands surrounded him
and Winnie hugged him.
Nelson looked into the sky
and smiled at the ancestors.
"*Amandla!* Thank you."
The sun sparkled in his gray and white hair.

Nelson stood proudly
with the wind at his back
and spoke to a colorful sea of people.
"We must forget our terrible past
and build a better future for South Africa.
Let us continue to fight for justice
and walk the last mile to freedom."

Millions were given the vote
and elected Nelson Mandela
their new leader.
South Africa was free at last
and finally at peace.
The ancestors,
The people,
The world,
Celebrated.

Amandla!
Ngawethu!

■ ■ ■ **NELSON MANDELA**

was born on July 18, 1918, in the Transkei region of South Africa. Nelson was the youngest son in a family of four boys and nine girls and was born with the name Rolihlahla, which translates as "troublemaker." However, his birth name was changed to Nelson on his first day of school.

When Nelson was nine years old, his father died. To continue his schooling, Nelson was sent miles away to live with a powerful chief named Jongitaba. During his time with the chief, Nelson began to learn about South African tribal history, politics, and diplomacy.

Nelson later studied law and joined the African National Congress (ANC) Youth League, a political organization, to fight against the new discriminatory apartheid laws enforced by the South African government. The laws segregated beaches, parks, and public institutions, making it so that white, Indian, and black Africans were not allowed to enjoy them together. Europeans Only signs were posted all over South Africa, igniting widespread protests and violence.

Nelson traveled the country to organize a resistance campaign to protest the new policy. This soon led to his arrest and brief imprisonment.

Nelson then opened what was to be South Africa's first black law firm in August 1952 in Johannesburg with colleague Oliver Tambo. As Nelson continued to participate in resistance campaigns with the ANC (which was soon declared illegal by the South African government), he was often arrested, banned, and imprisoned.

In the late 1950s, as a result of his involvement with the ANC, Nelson was accused of treason and put on trial with 156 other men. It was during this trial that Nelson met and married Winnie Madikizela. The trial was later dismissed, but Nelson was placed at the top of the government's most wanted list of political agitators. As a result, Nelson decided to go underground to lead the resistance campaign against apartheid. During this time, Nelson secretly left South Africa to visit other African and European countries to garner support for South Africa's resistance movement.

However, upon his return to South Africa, Nelson was captured, convicted, and sentenced to life imprisonment for illegally leaving the country and for his involvement in the resistance movement.

While Nelson sat in prison, South Africa became unstable with widespread violence and protests. South Africa, spurred by political pressure from other world nations, yearned for new leadership and ultimately declared apartheid illegal.

At long last, Nelson and his comrades were released in early 1990 after having spent more than twenty-seven years behind bars as political prisoners. Nelson was soon elected president of the ANC, and three years later he was awarded the Nobel Peace Prize (along with F. W. de Klerk, president of South Africa). One year later Nelson was inaugurated the first black president of South Africa in a landslide election. During his address to South Africa, Nelson spoke proudly:

"We understand it still that there is no easy road to freedom. We know it well that none of us acting alone can achieve success. We must therefore act together as a united people, for national reconciliation, for nation building, for the birth of a new world. Let there be justice for all. Let there be peace for all. Let there be work, bread, water, and salt for all. Let each know that for each the body, the mind, and the soul have been freed to fulfill themselves. Never, never, and never again shall it be that this beautiful land will again experience the oppression of one by another and suffer the indignity of being the skunk of the world. Let freedom reign."

–Kadir Nelson ■ ■ ■

■■■ BIBLIOGRAPHY ■■■

Cohen, David Elliot, and John D. Battersby. *Nelson Mandela: A Life in Photographs.* New York: Sterling Publishing, 2009.

Maharaj, Mac, and Ahmed Kathrada, eds. *Mandela: The Authorized Portrait.* Kansas City: Andrews McMeel Publishing, 2006.

Mandela, Nelson. *Long Walk to Freedom: The Autobiography of Nelson Mandela.* Boston: Little Brown, 1994.